INSTANT POT VEGAN

RECIPES

Matt Laurence

Table of Contents

INSTANT POT VEGAN SOUP

Pumpkin Coconut Soup

Serving: 3

Prep Time: 15 minutes

Cook Time: 25 minutes

Ingredients:

- 1 cup of pumpkin, diced
- 3 garlic cloves, minced
- 1 red pepper, chopped
- 1 red onion, chopped
- 2 teaspoon paprika
- 4 cups of vegetable broth
- 1 can of coconut milk
- 2 tablespoons coconut butter
- chives, red pepper and cilantro for garnish
- nutmeg

How to Prepare:

1. Boil the pumpkin to half-cooked and set aside.

2. Set your Instant Pot to sauté mode and stew the onion and garlic for 5 minutes until clear and caramelized, add ¼ cup of broth.
3. Add all the remaining ingredients and stir in the pumpkin.
4. Close the lid and cook on a MEDIUM pressure for 20 minutes.
5. Release the pressure naturally over 10 minutes.
6. Puree the vegetables using the blender.
7. Serve with the white bread and garnish with a bit of chives, red pepper, and cilantro.

Nutrition (Per Serving):

Calories: 167; Fat: 34g; Carbohydrates: 150g; Protein: 27g

Tomatocs and Pumpkin Soup with Basil

Serving: 3

Prep Time: 10 minutes

Cook Time: 30 minutes

Ingredients:

     a. 5 large tomatoes, quartered

     b. 2 cups of pumpkin, diced

     c. 2 onions, chopped

     d. 5 glasses of vegetable broth or water

     e. 1 bunch of chives, chopped

     f. 1 pinch of sea salt

     g. 4 tablespoons dried basil

How to Prepare:

- Blend the tomatoes for 5-10 minutes until there is smooth and frothy consistency.
- Place all the ingredients into your Instant Pot and close the lid to select the soup function.
- Cook the soup for 30 minutes.
- Use an immersion blender to blend the vegetables into a smooth mixture.
- Portion the tomatoes and pumpkin soup into three bowls or mugs and dollop each bowl with the chives. Remember that this dish should be served warm.

Nutrition (Per Serving):

Calories: 153; Fat: 35g; Carbohydrates: 154g; Protein: 27g

Dock, Celery and Spinach Soup

Serving: 2

Prep Time: 15 minute

Cooking Time: 25 minutes

Ingredients:

    a. 2 cups of dock, chopped

    b. 2 cups of spinach chopped

    c. 15 oz celery, diced

    d. 2 leeks, chopped

    e. 1 cup of Gouda cheese, grated

    f. 1/2 celeriac, peeled and diced

    g. 1 cup of potatoes, peeled and diced

    h. 1 cup of vegetable stock

    i. 1 cup of coconut milk

    j. Salt and pepper as needed

How to Prepare:

- Add all the listed ingredients (except the Gouda cheese) to your Instant Pot and stir gently.
- Close the lid and cook for 25 minutes on a HIGH pressure.
- Release the pressure over 10 minutes.
- Portion the soup into two bowls or mugs and dollop each bowl with the grated Gouda cheese and serve with the white bread or baguette.

Nutrition (Per Serving):

Calories: 154; Fat: 31g; Carbohydrates: 171g; Protein: 26g

Spicy Cabbage Soup

Serving: 3

Prep Time: 10 minutes

Cooking Time: 30 minutes

Ingredients:

a. 20 oz cabbage, diced

b. 10 oz celery, diced

c. 4 whole carrots, peeled and chopped

d. 3 garlic cloves, minced

e. 2 medium onions, peeled and chopped

f. 4 cups of vegetable stock, low sodium

g. 1/2 tablespoon of red curry paste

h. 1 tablespoon of cilantro, chopped

i. 1 teaspoon chili pepper

j. 1 cayenne pepper

How to Prepare:

- In a skillet, heat the oil and fry the carrots and onions until caramelized.
- Combine the squash, carrots, onions, garlic, spinach, stock, curry paste, cayenne, chili and cilantro in your Instant Pot and toss well.
- Close the lid and cook on a HIGH pressure for 30 minutes.
- Release the pressure naturally over 10 minutes.
- Portion the soup into three bowls or mugs and serve with the white wine.

Nutrition (Per Serving):

Calories: 162; Fat: 32g; Carbohydrates: 156g; Protein: 29g

Instant Cauliflower Soup with Cream

Serving: 3

Prep Time: 15 minutes

Cooking Time: 40 minutes

Ingredients:

1. 25 oz cauliflower, peeled and diced
2. 5 cloves of garlic, minced
3. 1 cup of vegan coconut cream
4. 4 cups of salted water
5. 2 tablespoons sunflower oil
6. 1 teaspoon dried parsley
7. 1 teaspoon cumin
8. 1 teaspoon turmeric
9. ¼ teaspoon paprika
10. 1 bunch of chives, chopped

How to Prepare:

- Boil the cauliflower for around 10 minutes until half-cooked.
- Place all the ingredients into your Instant Pot. Pour the salted water. Close the lid and select the soup function.
- Boil the soup on MEDIUM pressure for 30 minutes.
- Pour the vegan coconut cream and blend using an immersion blender.
- Ladle the soup into the three bowls or mugs and dollop each bowl with the chopped chives. Remember that this dish should be served warm.

Nutrition (Per Serving):

Calories: 152; Fat: 36g; Carbohydrates: 167g; Protein: 29g

Instant Potatoes Soup

Serving: 3

Prep Time: 15 minutes

Cooking Time: 40 minutes

<u>Ingredients:</u>

1. 15 oz potatoes, peeled and diced
2. 2 carrots, peeled and sliced
3. 5 cloves of garlic, minced
4. 4 cups of salted water
5. 2 tablespoons sunflower oil
6. 1 teaspoon dried parsley
7. 1 teaspoon cumin
8. 1 teaspoon turmeric
9. ¼ teaspoon paprika
10. fresh cilantro

How to Prepare:

- Place all the ingredients into your Instant Pot. Pour the salted water. Close the lid and select the soup function.
- Boil the soup on a MEDIUM pressure for 40 minutes.
- Portion the potatoes soup into three bowls or mugs and dollop each bowl with the basil. Remember that this dish should be served warm.

Nutrition (Per Serving):

Calories: 153; Fat: 37g; Carbohydrates: 165g; Protein: 34g

Instant Tomatoes Creamy Soup with Onions

Serving: 3

Prep Time: 10 minutes

Cook Time: 30 minutes

Ingredients:

1. 10 oz tomatoes, diced
2. 1 cup of tomato sauce
3. 4 onions, peeled
4. 3 cups of vegetable broth
5. 1 tablespoon salt
6. black pepper, to taste
7. 1 bunch of basil, chopped

How to Prepare:

- Blend the tomatoes for 5-10 minutes until there is smooth and frothy consistency.
- Place all the ingredients into your Instant Pot and close the lid to select the soup function.
- Boil the soup on a HIGH pressure for 30 minutes.
- Use an immersion blender to blend the tomatoes soup into a smooth mixture.
- Portion the tomatoes soup into three bowls or mugs and dollop each bowl with the basil. Remember that this dish should be served warm.

Nutrition (Per Serving):

Calories: 143; Fat: 31g; Carbohydrates: 154g; Protein: 32g

Instant Broccoli Soup with Bell Pepper

Serving: 3

Prep Time: 15 minutes

Cooking Time: 40 minutes

<u>Ingredients:</u>

1. 3 broccoli
2. 3 bell peppers, diced
3. 3 medium potatoes, peeled and diced
4. 1 carrot, peeled and sliced
5. 10 basil leaves, chopped
6. 5 cloves of garlic, minced
7. 4 cups of salted water
8. 2 tablespoons sunflower oil
9. 1 teaspoon dried parsley
10. 1 teaspoon cumin
11. 1 teaspoon paprika
12. ¼ teaspoon paprika

13. fresh cilantro

How to Prepare:

- Wash the broccoli well. Break the broccoli into the big florets by slicing straight through the broccoli stem. Then boil the broccoli for around 10 minutes until half-cooked.
- Place all the ingredients into your Instant Pot. Close the lid and select the soup function.
- Boil the soup on a MEDIUM pressure for 30 minutes.
- Portion the broccoli soup into three bowls or mugs and dollop each bowl with the basil. Remember that this dish should be served warm.

Nutrition (Per Serving):

Calories: 150; Fat: 35g; Carbohydrates: 164g; Protein: 32g

Zucchini Soup with Garlic

Serving: 4

Prep Time: 10 minutes

Cooking Time: 30 minutes

Ingredients:

1. 15 oz zucchini, diced
2. 4 whole carrots, peeled and chopped
3. 5 garlic cloves, minced
4. 2 medium onions, peeled and chopped
5. 4 cups of vegetable stock, low sodium
6. 1/2 tablespoon of red curry paste
7. 1 teaspoon paprika
8. 1 tablespoon of cilantro, chopped

How to Prepare:

- In a skillet, heat the oil and fry the carrots and onions until caramelized.
- Combine the zucchini, carrots, onions, garlic, vegetable stock, curry paste and cilantro in your Instant Pot and toss well.
- Close the lid and cook on a HIGH pressure for 30 minutes.
- Release the pressure naturally over 10 minutes.
- Blend using an immersion blender.
- Portion the soup into four bowls or mugs and serve with the white wine.

Nutrition (Per Serving):

Calories: 133; Fat: 20g; Carbohydrates: 141g; Protein: 22g

Celery Bouillon with Eggplant

Serving: 4

Prep Time: 10 minutes

Cooking Time: 40 minutes

Ingredients:

1. 30 oz celery
2. 20 oz eggplant, diced
3. 1 chili pepper
4. 3 tablespoons frozen vegetable mix
5. 5 cups of water
6. 3 teaspoons basil, dried and crushed
7. 1/8 teaspoon oregano, crushed
8. 1 medium onion, chopped
9. 6 garlic cloves, minced
10. sea salt and black pepper, to taste

How to Prepare:

- Add all the ingredients to the Instant Pot and mix well.
- Close the lid and select the slow mode to cook for 40 minutes.
- Keep the pressure and then release the handle to the Venting position.
- Once cooked, stir the bouillon well.
- Portion the bouillon into four bowls or mugs. Remember that this dish should be served warm.

Nutrition (Per Serving):

Calories: 215; Fat: 47g; Carbohydrates: 145g; Protein:

Broccoli and Leek Soup

Serving: 3

Prep Time: 15 minutes

Cooking Time: 40 minutes

Ingredients:

1. 1 broccoli, chopped
2. 2 leeks, chopped
3. 1 leek, chopped
4. ½ of yellow onion, chopped
5. 4 cloves of garlic, minced
6. 1 tablespoon curry powder
7. 1 teaspoon cayenne pepper
8. 4 cups of water
9. 2 cups of vegetable broth
10. fresh greenery, chopped

How to Prepare:

- Add the ¼ cup of water to the Instant Pot and set the Instant Pot to the sauté mode.

- Spoon the onions and garlic and sauté for 15 minutes until clear and caramelized.
- Add the vegetable broth, cayenne and curry powder, mix well.
- Pour the water and sauté for 5 minutes.
- Mix in all the remaining ingredients and close the lid.
- Cook on a HIGH pressure for 20 minutes.
- Release the pressure naturally. Portion the broccoli soup into three bowls or mugs and dollop each bowl with the fresh greenery. Remember that this dish should be served warm.

Nutrition (Per Serving):

Calories: 168; Fat: 36g; Carbohydrates: 155g; Protein: 31g

Cabbage Soup with Croutons

Serving: 4

Prep Time: 10 minutes

Cooking Time: 55 minutes

Ingredients:

1. 30 oz cabbage, chopped
2. 1 chili pepper
3. 3 tablespoons frozen vegetable mix
4. 1 baguette
5. 4 tablespoons Olive oil
6. 2 tablespoons garlic powder
7. 2 tablespoons herbs
8. 5 cups of water
9. 3 teaspoons basil, dried and crushed
10. 1/8 teaspoon oregano, crushed
11. 1 medium onion, chopped

12. 6 garlic cloves, minced

13. sea salt and black pepper, to taste

How to Prepare:

- Cut the baguette into the small cubes and toss them with the salt, Olive oil, herbs and garlic powder. Preheat the oven to 250°-270° Fahrenheit and spoon the baguette cubes on a baking sheet. Bake the croutons for 10-15 minutes until golden brown and crispy.

- Add all the ingredients to the Instant Pot (except the croutons) and mix well.

- Close the lid and select the slow mode to cook for 40 minutes.

- Keep the pressure and then release the handle to the Venting position.

- Once cooked, stir the soup well.

- Portion the soup into four bowls or mugs and dollop each bowl with the croutons. Remember that this dish should be served warm.

Nutrition (Per Serving):

Calories: 172; Fat: 42g; Carbohydrates: 138g; Protein: 32g

Spanish Soup with Squash

Serving: 4

Prep Time: 15 minutes

Cooking Time: 45 minutes

Ingredients:

1. 15 oz squash, diced
2. 4 tablespoon sunflower oil
3. 2 teaspoons chili pepper powder
4. 1 medium onion, thinly sliced
5. 2 garlic cloves, smashed
6. salt and pepper, to taste
7. 1 cup of vegetable stock
8. 5 cups of water
9. ¼ cup of cilantro for garnish
10. 1 teaspoon rosemary
11. 1 teaspoon laurel (also called bay leaf)
12. 1 teaspoon oregano
13. 1 teaspoon basil

14. 1 teaspoon thyme

15. 1 teaspoon mint

16. 1 bunch of parsley, chopped

17. 1 bunch of dill, chopped

How to Prepare:

- Set your Instant Pot to sauté mode and add some sunflower oil.
- Add the chili pepper powder and sauté for 5 minutes.
- Add the onion, 2 tablespoons of cilantro, garlic and season with the salt and pepper.
- Stir for a few minutes and add in the vegetable stock.
- Season the squash with the salt and pepper.
- In the Instant Pot, combine the ¼ cup of cilantro, 1 teaspoon rosemary, 1 teaspoon laurel (also called bay leaf), 1 teaspoon oregano, 1 teaspoon basil, 1 teaspoon thyme, 1 teaspoon mint, 1 bunch of parsley and all the remaining ingredients.
- Close the lid and cook on a LOW pressure for 40 minutes.
- Release the pressure over 10 minutes.

- Portion the soup into four bowls or mugs and dollop each bowl with the chopped dill. Remember that this dish should be served warm.

Nutrition (Per Serving):

Calories: 168; Fat: 41g; Carbohydrates: 152g; Protein: 32g

Potatoes and Squash Soup with Basil

Serving: 3

Prep Time: 10 minutes

Cook Time: 30 minutes

Ingredients:

a. 10 medium potatoes, quartered

b. 2 cups of squash, diced

c. 2 onions, chopped

d. 5 glasses of vegetable broth or water

e. 1 bunch of chives, chopped

f. 1 pinch of sea salt

g. 4 tablespoons dried basil

How to Prepare:

- Place all the ingredients into your Instant Pot and close the lid. Then select the soup function.
- Cook the soup for 30 minutes.
- Portion the soup into three bowls or mugs and dollop each bowl with the chives. Remember that this dish should be served warm.

Nutrition (Per Serving):

Calories: 153; Fat: 35g; Carbohydrates: 154g; Protein: 27g

Potatoes and Rice Milk Soup

Serving: 3

Prep Time: 8 minutes

Cook Time: 20 minutes

<u>Ingredients:</u>

    a. 4 cups of rice milk

    b. 4 potatoes, peeled and diced

    c. 3 carrots, peeled and diced

    d. 1 cup of water

    e. ½ teaspoon flavored apple vinegar

    f. 1 bunch of chives, chopped

<u>How to Prepare:</u>

- Add the potatoes, carrots and garlic to the Instant Pot. Pour the rice milk.
- Pour the water milk and some apple vinegar. Then close the lid and cook on a MEDIUM pressure for 20 minutes.
- Release the pressure naturally over 10 minutes and open the lid.
- Portion the soup into three bowls or mugs and dollop each bowl with the fresh and chopped chives. Remember that this dish should be served warm.

Nutrition (Per Serving):

Calories: 142; Fat: 27g; Carbohydrates: 130g; Protein: 23g

Instant Potatoes Soup

Serving: 4

Prep Time: 10 minutes

Cooking Time: 40 minutes

Ingredients:

    a. 20 oz potatoes, peeled and diced

    b. 1 chili pepper

    c. 3 carrots, peeled and diced

    d. 5 cups of vegetable broth

    e. 1 teaspoon oregano, crushed

    f. 3 medium onions, peeled and chopped

    g. 6 garlic cloves, minced

    h. 1 bunch of basil, chopped

    i. sea salt and black pepper, to taste

How to Prepare:

- Add all the ingredients to the Instant Pot and mix well.
- Close the lid and select the slow mode to cook for 40 minutes.
- Keep the pressure and then release the handle to the Venting position.
- Once cooked, stir the soup well.
- Portion the soup into four bowls or mugs. Remember that this dish should be served warm.

Nutrition (Per Serving):

Calories: 167; Fat: 32g; Carbohydrates: 168g; Protein: 22g

INSTANT POT
OTHER RECIPES

Instant Couscous with Raisins

Serving: 4

Prep Time: 25 minutes

Cooking Time: 30 minutes

Ingredients:

    a. 2 cups of couscous, rinsed

    b. 4 cups of water

    c. ¼ teaspoon salt

    d. 2 tablespoons brown sugar

    e. 1 cup of raisins

    f. 1 teaspoon cinnamon

    g. ¼ teaspoon citric acid

How to Prepare:

- Soak the raisins in the warm water for 10 minutes.
- Soak the couscous in the warm water for around 10-15 minutes. Mix in all the listed ingredients and spoon them to your Instant Pot. Then pour the water.
- Close the lid and cook on a MEDIUM pressure for 30 minutes.
- Release the pressure naturally over 10 minutes.
- Portion the couscous into four bowls or mugs. Remember that this dish should be served warm. Serve the couscous with the coffee.

Nutrition (Per Serving):

Calories: 107; Fat: 19g; Carbohydrates: 88g; Protein: 17g

Artichokes and Kale with Cashews

Serving: 3

Prep Time: 10 minutes

Cook Time: 30 minutes

Ingredients:

a. 1 cup of artichoke hearts

b. 1 tablespoon parsley, chopped

c. 1 cup of cashews

d. 1 cup of kale, torn

e. 1 cup of sunflower seeds

f. ½ tablespoon balsamic vinegar

g. 1 tablespoon olive oil

h. Salt and black pepper, to taste

How to Prepare:

- Preheat the oven to 250°-270° Fahrenheit and roast the cashews in the oven for 10 minutes until lightly browned and crispy and then set aside.

- Add all the ingredients (except the cashews) into your Pot and close the lid to cook on a MEDIUM pressure for around 20 minutes. Then release the pressure over 5 minutes.
- Portion the vegetables into three bowls or mugs and dollop each bowl with the cashews and serve with the white wine.

Nutrition (Per Serving):

Calories: 153; Fat: 28g; Carbohydrates: 132g; Protein: 25g

Cauliflower with Basil and Onion

Serving: 3

Prep Time: 15 minutes

Cooking Time: 25 minutes

Ingredients:

1. 1 large cauliflower head
2. 10 basil leaves, chopped
3. 4 onions, peeled and chopped
4. 4 cloves of garlic, minced
5. 2 tablespoons sunflower oil
6. 1 teaspoon salt
7. 1 teaspoon dried parsley
8. 1 teaspoon cumin
9. 1 teaspoon turmeric
10. ¼ teaspoon paprika

11. fresh cilantro

How to Prepare:

- Wash the cauliflower well and trim the leaves, then boil the cauliflower for around 10 minutes until half-cooked.
- Place a steamer rack on top of the Instant Pot and transfer the cauliflower to the rack.
- Add 1 cup of water into the Instant Pot.
- Close the lid and cook the cauliflower on a HIGH pressure for 15 minutes.
- Set your Instant Pot to the sauté mode and add in the oil and all the remaining ingredients. Allow the oil to heat up and cook the cauliflower for 10 minutes.
- Add the spices and season with a bit of salt.
- Portion the cauliflower into three bowls or mugs and dollop each bowl with the basil. Remember that this dish should be served warm.

Nutrition (Per Serving):

Calories: 142; Fat: 33g; Carbohydrates: 162g; Protein: 28g

Pears and Orange Marmalade Quinoa

Serving: 2

Prep Time: 10 minutes

Cooking Time: 25 minutes

Ingredients:

1. 1 cup of quinoa, rinsed
2. 5 oz orange marmalade, diced
3. 2 cups of water
4. 4 sour-sweet pears, seeded and diced
5. 2 oranges, diced
6. 2 tablespoons white sugar
7. 3 teaspoons vanilla
8. ¼ teaspoon citric acid

How to Prepare:

- Sprinkle the diced pears with the vanilla and citric acid and place them in the fridge for 10 minutes.
- Heat the water and then soak the quinoa in the warm water for around 10-15 minutes. Add all the listed ingredients to your Instant Pot and pour the water.
- Close the lid and cook on a MEDIUM pressure for 25 minutes.
- Release the pressure naturally over 10 minutes.
- Portion the pears and vanilla quinoa mix into two bowls or mugs and dollop each bowl with the white sugar and orange marmalade. Remember that this dish should be served warm. Serve the pears quinoa with the cappuccino.

Nutrition (Per Serving):

Calories: 166; Fat: 25g; Carbohydrates: 35g; Protein: 19g

Blueberries Oats with Almond Milk and Banana

Serving: 3

Prep Time: 10-15 minutes

Cooking Time: 30 minutes

Ingredients:

1. 3 cups of oats
2. 2 bananas, diced
3. 1 cup of fresh blueberries
4. 1 cup of raisins
5. 4 cups of almond milk
6. ¼ cup of maple syrup
7. 1 teaspoon vanilla extract

How to Prepare:

- In a bowl, combine the maple syrup, almond milk and vanilla extract and mix well until there is a smooth consistency and homogenous mass, then combine with the oats in your Instant Pot. Spoon the raisins.

- Close the lid and cook on a LOW pressure for around 30 minutes.
- Quick-release the pressure. Portion the oats into bowls or mugs and dollop each bowl with the fresh berries and banana. Remember that this dish should be served warm. Enjoy!

Nutrition (Per Serving):

Calories: 135; Fat: 19g; Carbohydrates: 26g; Protein: 14g

Millet with Cashews and Melon

Serving: 4

Prep Time: 10 minutes

Cook Time: 30 minutes

Ingredients:

1. 2 cups of millet, rinsed
2. 10 oz melon, cubed
3. 1 cup of cashews
4. 3 cups of oat milk
5. 2 tablespoons brown sugar
6. 2 bananas, peeled and sliced
7. ½ teaspoon cinnamon

How to Prepare:

- In a bowl, sprinkle the pears with the cinnamon.
- Soak the millet in the warm water for around 10 minutes. Then add in the millet to your pot.
- Pour the oat milk to your pot and stir well.

- Close the lid and cook on a LOW pressure for around 30 minutes.
- Release the pressure naturally over 10 minutes.
- Portion the millet into four bowls or mugs and dollop each bowl with some melon and cashews. Remember that this dish should be served warm. Serve the millet with the orange juice.

Nutrition (Per Serving):

Calories: 143; Fat: 24g; Carbohydrates: 114g; Protein: 24g

Coconut Taste Pineapples with Peach Jam

Serving: 4

Prep Time: 10-15 minutes

Cooking Time: 30 minutes

Ingredients:

1. 2 pineapples, peeled and diced
2. 1 cup of peach jam
3. ¼ cup of maple syrup
4. 4 tablespoons coconut butter
5. 1 teaspoon strawberry extract
6. 1 cup of coconut milk
7. 1 cup of cashews

How to Prepare:

- In a bowl, combine the maple syrup, coconut butter and strawberry extract and mix well until there is a smooth consistency and homogenous mass, then add in the pineapples. Spoon all the ingredients (except the cashews and jam) to your Instant Pot and toss. Pour the coconut milk.
- Close the lid and cook on a LOW pressure for 20 minutes.
- Quick-release the pressure. Portion the pineapple breakfast mix into four bowls or mugs and dollop each bowl with the cashews and peach jam. Remember that this dish should be served warm. Enjoy!

Nutrition (Per Serving):

Calories: 112; Fat: 14g; Carbohydrates: 82g; Protein: 15g

Blueberries-Peach Mix

Serving: 2

Prep Time: 10-15 minutes

Cooking Time: 20 minutes

Ingredients:

1. 2 cups of fresh blueberries
2. 1 tablespoon pure peach extract
3. ¼ cup of maple syrup
4. 4 tablespoons almond butter
5. ½ teaspoon almond extract
6. 4 tablespoons sugar
7. chocolate spray cream

How to Prepare:

- Cover the blueberries with the sugar and set aside for 10 minutes.
- In a bowl, combine the blueberries, pure peach extract, maple syrup, almond butter and almond

extract and mix well, then add in all the ingredients to your Instant Pot and toss.

- Close the lid and cook on a HIGH pressure for 20 minutes.
- Quick-release the pressure.
- Portion the blueberry mix into two bowls or mugs and dollop each bowl with the chocolate spray cream. Remember that this dish should be served warm with the cappuccino and baguette.

Nutrition (Per Serving):

Calories: 126; Fat: 14g; Carbohydrates: 24g; Protein: 15g

Caramelized Onions with Chili and Potatoes

Serving: 3

Prep Time: 10 minutes

Cooking Time: 60 minutes

Ingredients:

1. 5 potatoes, peeled and diced
2. 5 big onions, peeled and sliced
3. 5 garlic cloves, minced
4. 4 tablespoons white flour
5. 2 tablespoons water
6. 6 tablespoons Olive oil
7. 2 teaspoons chili pepper powder
8. 1 teaspoon salt
9. pepper to taste

How to Prepare:

- Set your Instant Pot to the sauté mode and adjust the heat to Medium, pre-heat the inner pot for 5 minutes. Add in the Olive oil, potatoes and garlic to stew for 10 minutes until clear and caramelized. Then pour the water, spoon the white flour, add in the salt and pepper, and stir well. Close the lid, making sure that the pressure valve is locked.
- Cook on a HIGH pressure for 30 minutes and quick-release the pressure.
- In a skillet, heat the oil and fry the onions on a low heat for 15 minutes until clear.
- Open the lid and set the pot to sauté mode to cook for about 10-15 minutes until the liquid is almost gone. Portion the vegetables into three bowls or mugs and dollop each bowl with the onions and chili pepper powder.

Nutrition (Per Serving):

Calories: 154; Fat: 25g; Carbohydrates: 160g; Protein: 24g

Lasagna with Marinara Sauce and Carrots

Serving: 3

Prep Time: 10 minutes

Cook Time: 45 minutes

Ingredients:

1. 2 cups of vegan cheese, grated
2. 1 pound pumpkin, sliced
3. 1 teaspoon fennel seeds
4. ½ teaspoon pressed garlic
5. 15 oz carrots, peeled and chopped
6. 1 cup of Marinara sauce
7. 20 oz noodles
8. 10 tablespoons Olive oil
9. ½ teaspoon fresh ground black pepper

How to Prepare:

- Boil the water and cook the noodles or pasta for 10-15 minutes or follow the cooking time suggested on the packet. Add 1 tablespoon Olive oil.
- In a bowl, combine the pumpkin, fennel seeds and garlic.
- Assemble lasagna by lightly coating bottom of 1-quart baking dish with the oil and spread a spoonful of Marinara sauce over the bottom.
- Add a layer of pasta, overlapping as little as possible, making sure to trim the edges to fit.
- Spoon more marinara sauce and pumpkin over the noodles.
- Spoon the half of the carrots over the sauce and dust with the grated vegan cheese.
- Repeat the process and top the last layer with the vegan cheese, place square aluminum foil over the top and crimp lightly.
- Pour 1 cup of water into the inner pot. Place reversible rack in power in lower position and place the baking dish on top.

- Close the lid and seal the valve, select the HIGH pressure and cook for 10 minutes.
- Select the Bake/Roast mode and cook for 35 minutes (350 F).
- Once the lasagna is browned and bubbling let it cool and portion the lasagna into three plates.

Nutrition (Per Serving):

Calories: 186; Fat: 40g; Carbohydrates: 154g; Protein: 32g

Spicy Fava Beans with Cheese

Serving: 3

Prep Time: 15 minutes

Cook Time: 20 minutes

Ingredients:

1. 1 cup of fava beans, canned
2. 1 cup of vegan or goat cheese, grated
3. 2 garlic cloves, minced
4. 1 tablespoon Olive oil
5. 1 tablespoon chili powder
6. salt and black pepper, to taste

How to Prepare:

- Set your Instant Pot on sauté mode.
- Add the Olive oil, heat it up and then mix in the garlic and chili powder, sauté for 5 minutes until clear.

- Add in the fava beans, salt, pepper and chili powder.
- Close the lid and cook on a HIGH pressure for 20 minutes.
- Release the pressure naturally over 5 minutes.
- Portion the spicy fava beans into three bowls or plates and dollop each plate with the cheese and serve with the white wine.

Nutrition (Per Serving):

Calories: 135; Fat: 29g; Carbohydrates: 119g; Protein: 23g

Squash with Carrots and Potatoes

Serving: 2

Prep Time: 5 minutes

Cook Time: 25 minutes

Ingredients:

    a. 20 oz squash, peeled and diced

    b. 10 carrots, peeled and chopped

    c. 2 potatoes, peeled and diced

    d. 10 oz celery, chopped

    e. 5 tablespoon tomato sauce

    f. 3 tablespoons white flour

    g. ½ teaspoon cumin seeds

    h. 4 garlic cloves, chopped

    i. 4 tablespoons pumpkin seeds oil

    j. Cilantro for garnish

    k. 1 teaspoon turmeric

    l. ½ a teaspoon cayenne pepper

m. 2 teaspoons coriander

n. 4 tablespoons lemon juice

How to Prepare:

- Set the Instant Pot to the sauté mode and add in the pumpkin seeds oil, then heat up the oil.

- Mix in the garlic and cumin and stew for 5 minutes until clear.

- Add in the squash, carrots, potatoes, celery, spices, flour and all the remaining ingredients. Mix well.

- Pour some water and close the lid to cook on a HIGH pressure for 20 minutes.

- Release the pressure naturally and add in the lemon juice.

- Mix well and portion the stewed vegetables into two plates and sprinkle each plate with the cilantro. Remember that this dish should be served warm. Serve the vegetables with the white bread and peanut butter.

Nutrition (Per Serving):

Calories: 138; Fat: 32g; Carbohydrates: 164g; Protein: 32g

Broccoli with Walnuts

Serving: 2

Prep Time: 5 minutes

Cooking Time: 30 minutes

Ingredients:

    a. 1 pound broccoli

    b. 1 cup of walnuts

    c. 1 tablespoon sesame seeds oil

    d. 1 teaspoon each pepper and salt

    e. 1 cup of water with the lime juice

How to Prepare:

- Preheat the oven to 250°-270°Fahrenheit and roast the walnuts in the oven for 5-10 minutes until lightly browned and crispy and then set aside to cool completely.

- Add the trivet to the Instant Pot and place a steamer on top.

- Add a cup of water with the lime juice.

- Place the broccoli into a steamer plate and close the lid to cook on a HIGH pressure for 20 minutes.
- Quick-release the pressure. Toss the broccoli in the sesame seeds oil.
- Season with the salt and pepper.
- Portion the broccoli into two plates and dollop each plate with the walnuts. Remember that this dish should be served warm. Serve the broccoli with the salad.

Nutrition (Per Serving):

Calories: 131; Fat: 33g; Carbohydrates: 110g; Protein: 26g

Millet with Pineapple

Serving: 2

Prep Time: 15 minutes

Cook Time: 25 minutes

Ingredients:

 a. 1 cup of millet
 b. 1 cup of pineapple, diced
 c. 1 cup of raisins
 d. 1 cup of dried apricots
 e. 5 garlic cloves, minced
 f. 1 red pepper, chopped
 g. 1 red onion, chopped
 h. 2 teaspoon paprika
 i. 4 cups of vegetable broth
 j. 1 can coconut milk
 k. chives, red pepper and cilantro for garnish
 l. nutmeg

How to Prepare:

- Wash and soak the raisins with the apricots in the warm water for around 10 minutes. Then chop the apricots.
- Boil the millet to half-cooked and set aside.
- Set your Instant Pot to sauté mode and stew the onion and garlic for 5 minutes until clear and caramelized, add ¼ cup of broth.
- Add all the remaining ingredients and stir in the millet.
- Close the lid and cook on a MEDIUM pressure for 20 minutes
- Release the pressure naturally over 10 minutes
- Portion the millet into two plates and dollop each plate with the nutmeg.
- Serve the millet and garnish with a bit of chives, red pepper and cilantro.

Nutrition (Per Serving):

Calories: 164; Fat: 28g; Carbohydrates: 145g; Protein: 27g

Oatmeal with Bananas and Strawberries

Serving: 3

Prep Time: 5 minutes

Cook Time: 20 minutes

Ingredients:

    a. 3 cups of oatmeal

    b. 3 bananas, sliced

    c. 1 cup of strawberries

    d. 1 mango, diced

    e. 1 cup of water

    f. 1 cup of rice milk

    g. 2 tablespoons brown sugar

    h. ½ teaspoon cinnamon

How to Prepare:

- Add in all the ingredients to your Instant Pot (except the bananas and berries).
- Close the lid of the Pot and press the Manual key to cook on a MEDIUM pressure for 20 minutes.
- Once cooked, release the pressure naturally and open the lid.
- Portion the oatmeal into three bowls or mugs and dollop each bowl with the bananas and berries. Remember that this dish should be served warm. Serve the oatmeal with the apple juice.

Nutrition (Per Serving):

Calories: 161; Fat: 26g; Carbohydrates: 93g; Protein: 23g

Oatmeal with Raisins

Serving: 3

Prep Time: 10 minutes

Cook Time: 25 minutes

Ingredients:

1. 1 cup of oats
2. 1 cup of raisins
3. 1 cup of water
4. 1 cup of almond milk
5. 1 tablespoon flaxseeds, ground
6. 1/2 teaspoon vanilla

How to Prepare:

- Soak the flaxseeds in the warm water for overnight.
- In a bowl, combine the water, oats, almond milk and flaxseeds and add them to your Instant Pot. Mix well.

- Close the lid and cook on a MEDIUM pressure for 25 minutes and then release the pressure naturally and open the lid. Mix in the raisins.
- Portion the oatmeal into three bowls or mugs and dollop each bowl with the vanilla. Remember that this dish should be served warm. Serve the oatmeal with the cocoa.

Nutrition (Per Serving)

Calories: 144; Fat: 21g; Carbohydrates: 28g; Protein: 18g

Banana Puree with Mango and Vanilla

Serving: 2

Prep Time: 15 minute

Cooking Time: 10 minutes

Ingredients:

1. 4 bananas, seeded and diced
2. 1 cup of mango, diced
3. 4 tablespoons cherry jam
4. 1 cup of water
5. 1 teaspoon vanilla

How to Prepare:

- Add the water to your Pot and place the steamer rack at the bottom of your pot.
- Spoon the bananas and mango in a steamer basket and place it on top of the steamer rack

and close the lid to cook on a HIGH pressure for 10 minutes.

- Quick-release the pressure and let the fruits to cool, mix in the vanilla and jam.
- Mash the fruits using the potato masher and season with the sugar to taste.
- Portion the fruits puree into two bowls, mugs or glasses. Remember that this dish should be served warm. Serve the fruits puree with the cherry jam.

Nutrition (Per Serving):

Calories: 117; Fat: 16g; Carbohydrates: 27g; Protein: 15g

Squash Halves with Cheese

Serving: 2
Prep Time: 10 minutes
Cook Time: 25 minutes

Ingredients:

1. 1 medium-sized squash, halved
2. 1 cup of water
3. 15 oz cherry tomatoes
4. 1 cup of black olives, pitted and sliced
5. 1 cup of vegan cheese, grated
6. 1 cup of marinated black olives, pitted and chopped
7. 5-7 garlic cloves, sliced
8. 5 tablespoons Olive oil
9. 1 teaspoon salt
10. 5 fresh basil leaves

How to Prepare:

- Halve the squash and scoop out the seeds.
- Meanwhile, in a skillet or wok, heat the Olive oil and stew the garlic for 5 minutes until clear. Add in the water to the Instant Pot and place a trivet on top.
- Place the squash halves on the trivet. The flesh side facing up. Add in the tomatoes. Close the lid and cook on a HIGH pressure for 15 minutes. Once the cooking is done, allow the pressure to release naturally. In a bowl, combine the cheese and all the remaining ingredients (except the tomatoes). Add a spoonful of vegan cheese mixture into each zucchini half and stew for 5-10 minutes to melt the cheese.
- Portion the squash into three plates and dollop each plate with the basil. Remember that this dish should be served warm.

Nutrition (Per Serving):

Calories: 165; Fat: 32g; Carbohydrates: 179g; Protein: 24g

Squash and Onions with Curry

Serving: 3

Prep Time: 15 minute

Cooking Time: 40 minutes

Ingredients:

1. 20 oz squash, peeled and diced
2. 2 cups of dock, chopped
3. 2 tablespoons curry
4. 2 medium onions, peeled and chopped
5. 2 leeks, chopped
6. 1 cup of vegan cheese, grated
7. 1/2 celeriac, peeled and diced
8. 1 cup of potatoes, peeled and diced
9. 1 cup of vegetable stock
10. 1 cup of water
11. Salt and pepper as needed

How to Prepare:

- Add all the listed ingredients (except the cheese) to your Instant Pot and stir gently.
- Close the lid and stew on a MEDIUM pressure for 40 minutes.
- Release the pressure over 10 minutes.
- Portion the vegetables into three bowls or mugs and dollop each bowl with the grated vegan cheese and serve with the white bread.

Nutrition (Per Serving):

Calories: 162; Fat: 31g; Carbohydrates: 131g; Protein: 27g

Spicy Red Beans with Corns and Potatoes

Serving: 3

Prep Time: 15 minutes

Cook Time: 70 minutes

Ingredients:

- 1 cup of red beans
- 10 medium potatoes, diced
- 1 cup of corns
- 1 cup of tomato sauce
- 3 cups of water
- 2 garlic cloves, minced
- 1 tablespoon Olive oil
- 1 tablespoon chili powder
- salt and black pepper, to taste
- spinach, chopped

How to Prepare:

1. Soak the beans in the warm water for overnight (8-12 hours).
2. Set your Instant Pot on sauté mode.
3. Add in the Olive oil, heat it up and then mix in the garlic and chili powder, sauté for 5 minutes until clear.
4. Add in the beans, corns, potatoes, tomato sauce, water, salt, pepper and chili powder.
5. Close the lid and cook on a MEDIUM pressure for 1 hour.
6. Release the pressure naturally over 5 minutes.
7. Portion the spicy beans into three bowls or plates and dollop each plate with the spinach and serve with the white wine.

Nutrition (Per Serving):

Calories: 135; Fat: 25g; Carbohydrates: 121g; Protein: 22g

Golden Nugget with Oranges and Pineapples

Serving: 4

Prep Time: 25 minutes

Cooking Time: 65 minutes

Ingredients:

1. 20 oz potatoes, diced
2. 20 oz golden nugget pumpkin, diced
3. 2 oranges, peeled and diced
4. 2 cups of pineapple, diced
5. 1 garlic clove, minced
6. 1 medium onion, chopped
7. 2 medium carrots, chopped
8. 1 bunch of parsley, chopped
9. 1 tablespoon thyme
10. 1 a cup of vegetable stock
11. ½ cup red wine
12. ½ a tablespoon Olive oil
13. salt and pepper to taste

How to Prepare:

- In a bowl, combine the garlic, parsley, salt and pepper. Toss the potatoes and pumpkin in the spices mix. Then pour the wine on top and set the vegetables aside to marinate them for at least few hours unrefrigerated at room temperature or place in the fridge overnight.
- Set your pot to sauté mode and pour the oil, allow the oil to heat up.
- Spoon the potatoes and golden nugget pumpkin cubes and cook for 15 minutes.
- Transfer the vegetables into a plate.
- Add in the onion and carrots and sauté for 5-10 minutes until translucent and caramelized. Then mix in all the vegetables and all the remaining ingredients to sauté for 20 minutes.
- Close the lid and cook on a HIGH pressure for 20 minutes.
- Release the pressure naturally over 10 minutes.
- Then portion the vegetables into four plates. Remember that this dish should be served warm. Serve it with the beer.

Nutrition (Per Serving):

Calories: 194; Fat: 29g; Carbohydrates: 155g; Protein: 23g

Zucchini and Sweet Potatoes with Cream

Serving: 2

Prep Time: 10 minutes

Cooking Time: 50 minutes

Ingredients:

1. 20 oz sweet potatoes, peeled and diced
2. 1 medium zucchini, peeled and diced
3. 4 tablespoons dried sage
4. 5 tablespoons vegan cream
5. 2 tablespoons Olive oil
6. 2 teaspoons dried thyme
7. 2 teaspoons ground cinnamon
8. 1 cup of vegetable broth
9. 1 teaspoon of salt
10. 1 teaspoon pepper

How to Prepare:

- First, set your Instant Pot to sauté mode and heat the oil or use the skillet to heat the oil and then pour it into your Instant Pot.
- In a bowl, combine the salt, pepper, dried thyme, sage and cinnamon. Season the sweet potatoes with the spices mix and toss it in the oil to cook for 10 minutes.
- Then, add in the zucchini and pour in the vegetable broth.
- Close the lid and cook on a MEDIUM pressure for about 40 minutes.
- Quick-release the pressure and transfer the vegetables to the plates. Ladle up the sauce (if any) and cream all over the vegetables. Remember that this dish should be served warm. Serve it with the cold beer.

Nutrition (Per Serving):

Calories: 166; Fat: 34g; Carbohydrates: 142g; Protein: 26g

Spicy Instant Zucchini with Cashews

Serving: 2

Prep Time: 15 minutes

Cooking Time: 55 minutes

Ingredients:

1. 25 oz zucchini, diced
2. ½ large onion, chopped
3. 1 cup of cashews
4. 1 garlic clove, minced
5. 1 bay leaf
6. 2 ounces tomato sauce
7. 1 tablespoon olives, pitted
8. 1 tablespoon cilantro, chopped
9. ½ cup of water
10. 2 teaspoon chili powder
11. Salt and pepper, to taste

How to Prepare:

- Preheat the oven to 240°-260°Fahrenheit and roast the cashews in the oven for 10 minutes until lightly browned and crispy and then set aside to cool completely. Then grind the cashews using a food processor or blender.
- Marinate the zucchini in the salt, pepper and chili powder for at least few hours unrefrigerated at room temperature or place in the fridge overnight. Set the Instant Pot to sauté mode and add in the zucchini. Cook it until lightly browned.
- Add in all the remaining ingredients and mix well.
- Close the lid and cook on a MEDIUM pressure for 45 minutes.
- Then portion the zucchini into two plates. Remember that this dish should be served warm. Serve it with the salad and brown rice.

Squash and String Beans

Serving: 3

Prep Time: 15 minutes

Cooking Time: 40 minutes

<u>Ingredients:</u>

1. 25 oz squash, sliced
2. 10 oz string beans
3. 2 teaspoons pepper
4. 4 medium carrots, peeled and chopped
5. 1 medium shallot, chopped
6. 3 teaspoons dried rosemary
7. 4 teaspoons garlic, minced
8. ¼ cup of vegetable broth
9. 4 tablespoons Olive oil
10. soy sauce, to taste

<u>How to Prepare:</u>

- In a bowl, combine the pepper, dried rosemary and garlic. Toss the squash in the spices mix and pour the oil over it. Then set the squash aside to marinate for at least few hours unrefrigerated at room temperature or place in the fridge overnight.
- Combine all the ingredients in your Instant Pot and close the lid to let them cook on a MEDIUM pressure for about 40 minutes.
- Release the pressure quickly.
- Divide the vegetables into three plates and pour the soy sauce on top to serve.

Nutrition (Per Serving):

Calories: 165; Fat: 34g; Carbohydrates: 119g; Protein: 27g

Broccoli with Squash and Spinach

Serving: 2

Prep Time: 15 minutes

Cooking Time: 40 minutes

<u>Ingredients:</u>

1. 1 medium broccoli, sliced
2. 1 medium squash, chopped
3. 20 oz spinach, chopped
4. 1 avocado, sliced
5. 2 cucumbers, sliced
6. ½ of yellow onion, chopped
7. 3 garlic cloves, minced
8. 1 tablespoon of curry powder
9. 1 teaspoon of cayenne pepper
10. 4 cups of water
11. 2 cups of vegetable broth
12. fresh greenery, chopped

How to Prepare:

- Add the ¼ cup of water to the Instant Pot and set the Instant Pot to the sauté mode.
- Spoon in the onions and garlic and sauté for 15 minutes until clear and caramelized.
- Ladle the vegetable broth, cayenne and curry powder, mix well.
- Add the water and sauté for 5 minutes.
- Add all the remaining ingredients (except the avocado, spinach and cucumbers) and close the lid.
- Cook on a HIGH pressure for 20 minutes. Release the pressure naturally. Add in the avocado and cucumbers.
- Portion the broccoli into two bowls or mugs and dollop each bowl with the fresh greenery. Remember that this dish should be served warm.

Nutrition (Per Serving):

Calories: 162; Fat: 34g; Carbohydrates: 141g; Protein: 32g

Pumpkin and Coconut Milk

Serving: 2

Prep Time: 8 minutes

Cook Time: 20 minutes

Ingredients:

1. 1 pound pumpkin, peeled and diced
2. 3 carrots, peeled and diced
3. 5 garlic cloves, peeled
4. 2 teaspoons garlic powder
5. 1 cup of coconut milk
6. ½ teaspoon flavored vinegar
7. 1 bunch of chives, chopped

How to Prepare:

- Combine the coconut milk, pumpkin and garlic and add to the Instant Pot.
- Close the lid and cook on a HIGH pressure for 20 minutes.
- Release the pressure naturally over 10 minutes.
- Mash the pumpkin using a potato masher. Then stir in the flavored vinegar.
- Portion the pumpkin into two bowls or mugs and dollop each bowl with the fresh and chopped chives. Remember that this dish should be served warm.

Nutrition (Per Serving):

Calories: 152; Fat: 32g; Carbohydrates: 131g; Protein: 21g

Potatoes with Dill and Parsley

Serving: 2

Prep Time: 10 minutes

Cooking Time: 30 minutes

Ingredients:

1. 20 oz potatoes, peeled and halved
2. 1 tablespoon sunflower oil
3. 2 tablespoons soy sauce
4. 1 teaspoon salt
5. 1 cup of water
6. 1 bunch of dill, chopped
7. 1 bunch of parsley, chopped

How to Prepare:

- Combine the dill and parsley. Spoon some salt and mix well.
- Add all the listed ingredients (except the oil, soy sauce, parsley and dill) to the Instant Pot.

- Close the lid and cook on MEAT/STEW mode for 30 minutes.
- Release the pressure naturally over 10 minutes.
- Portion the halved potatoes into two plates and dollop each plate with the parsley, dill, soy sauce and oil. Remember that this dish should be served warm.

Nutrition (Per Serving):

Calories: 159; Fat: 28g; Carbohydrates: 118g; Protein: 23g

Pumpkin with Apricots and Oats

Serving: 2

Prep Time: 15 minutes

Cook Time: 35 minutes

<u>Ingredients:</u>

1. 1 cup of pumpkin, cubed
2. 1 cup of apricots
3. 4 tablespoons raisins
4. 1 cup of oats
5. 3 garlic cloves, minced
6. 1 red pepper, chopped
7. 1 red onion, chopped
8. 2 teaspoon paprika
9. 1 can of coconut milk
10. Vinegar as needed
11. chives, red pepper and cilantro for garnish
12. nutmeg

How to Prepare:

- Wash and soak the oats in the warm water for 20 minutes.
- Boil the oats to half-cooked and set aside.
- Set your Instant Pot to sauté mode and stew the onion and garlic for 5 minutes until clear and caramelized, add ¼ cup of broth.
- Add the oats and all the remaining ingredients.
- Close the lid and cook on a MEDIUM pressure for 20-30 minutes.
- Release the pressure naturally over 10 minutes. Blend the pumpkin and oats.
- Serve with the white bread and garnish with a bit of chives, red pepper, and cilantro.

Nutrition (Per Serving):

Calories: 163; Fat: 32g; Carbohydrates: 155g; Protein: 32g

Pumpkin with Buckwheat and Onions

Serving: 2

Prep Time: 10 minute

Cook Time: 40 minutes

Ingredients:

1. 20 oz pumpkin, peeled and cubed
2. 5 tablespoons garlic powder
3. 1 cup of buckwheat
4. salt and pepper to taste
5. 4 onions, peeled and chopped
6. 1 cup of water

How to Prepare:

- Combine all the ingredients in your Instant Pot.
- Cook on a HIGH pressure for 30 minutes.
- Quick-release the pressure.

- Close the lid and cook the pumpkin on Air Crisp mode for 10 minutes.
- Portion the pumpkin into two bowls or mugs and dollop each bowl with the salt and pepper. Remember that this dish should be served warm.

Nutrition (Per Serving):

Calories: 143; Fat: 30g; Carbohydrates: 158g; Protein: 24g

Squash with Lemon

Serving: 2

Prep Time: 10 minutes

Cook Time: 30 minutes

<u>Ingredients:</u>

1. 5 large tomatoes, quartered
2. 15 oz squash, diced
3. 2 lemons, diced
4. 2 onions, chopped
5. 2 cups of vegetable broth
6. 1 bunch of chives, chopped
7. 1 pinch of sea salt
8. 4 tablespoons dried basil
9. 3 tablespoons lemon juice

<u>How to Prepare:</u>

- Blend the tomatoes for 5-10 minutes until there is smooth and frothy consistency.
- Place all the ingredients into your Instant Pot and close the lid.
- Cook on a HIGH pressure for 30 minutes.
- Use an immersion blender to blend the tomatoes and squash into a smooth mixture.
- Portion the tomatoes and squash into two bowls or mugs and dollop each bowl with the chives and lemon juice. Remember that this dish should be served warm.

Nutrition (Per Serving):

Calories: 149; Fat: 33g; Carbohydrates: 125g; Protein: 28g

Cauliflower with Hazelnuts

Serving: 3

Prep Time: 15 minutes

Cooking Time: 25 minutes

Ingredients:

1. 1 large cauliflower head
2. 1 cup of hazelnuts
3. 5 cloves of garlic, minced
4. 2 tablespoons sunflower oil
5. 1 teaspoon salt
6. 1 teaspoon dried parsley
7. 1 teaspoon cumin
8. 2 oranges, peeled and diced
9. 1 teaspoon turmeric
10. ¼ teaspoon paprika
11. fresh cilantro

How to Prepare:

- Wash the cauliflower well and trim the leaves, then boil the cauliflower for around 10 minutes until half-cooked.
- Place a steamer rack on top of the Instant Pot and transfer the cauliflower to the rack.
- Add 1 cup of water into the Instant Pot.
- Close the lid and cook the cauliflower on a HIGH pressure for 15 minutes.
- Set your Instant Pot to the sauté mode and add in the oil and all the remaining ingredients (except the hazelnuts). Allow the oil to heat up and cook the cauliflower for 10 minutes.
- Add the spices and season with a bit of salt.
- Portion the cauliflower into three bowls or mugs and dollop each bowl with the hazelnuts. Remember that this dish should be served warm.

Nutrition (Per Serving):

Calories: 158; Fat: 38g; Carbohydrates: 111g; Protein: 23g

Spicy Carrots with Sunflower Seeds

Serving: 2

Prep Time: 15 minutes

Cooking Time: 20 minutes

Ingredients:

1. 10 carrots, peeled and chopped
2. 4 potatoes, peeled and cubed
3. 1 cup of sunflower seeds
4. 2 tablespoons tomato sauce
5. 1 tablespoon apple cider vinegar
6. ½ cup of applesauce
7. 1 cup of water
8. 2 garlic cloves, minced
9. 1 small onion, peeled and chopped
10. 1 tablespoon Olive oil
11. 1 teaspoon chili pepper powder
12. salt and pepper to taste

13. 1 bunch of parsley, chopped

How to Prepare:

- In a skillet, bake the sunflower seeds on a low heat for around 10 minutes until lightly brown.
- Spoon the Olive oil into your Instant Pot and set it to the sauté mode and let it heat up, add in the onion and garlic and sauté for 5-10 minutes until clear and caramelized.
- Add all the remaining ingredients and mix well.
- Close the lid and cook on a HIGH pressure for 10 minutes.
- Quick-release the pressure.
- Portion the carrots into two bowls or mugs and dollop each bowl with the chopped parsley and sunflower seeds. Serve the dish with the white wine.

Nutrition (Per Serving):

Calories: 156; Fat: 32g; Carbohydrates: 125g; Protein: 24g

Instant Vegan Burgers

Serving: 4

Prep Time: 10 minutes

Cooking Time: 55 minutes

Ingredients:

1. 4 buns, halved
2. 2 tomatoes, sliced
3. 2 carrots, chopped
4. 1 daikon, sliced
5. 1 white onion, peeled and sliced
6. 4 oz vegan cheese, sliced
7. 3 tablespoons soy sauce
8. 10 oz lettuce
9. 1 tablespoon Olive oil
10. 4 tablespoons vegan mayonnaise
11. salt and black pepper, to taste

How to Prepare:

- Preheat the oven to 250°-270°Fahrenheit and roast the buns in the oven for 10 minutes until lightly browned and crispy and then set aside.
- Add the carrots to your Pot and pour some oil. Close the lid to cook on MEAT/STEW mode. Set the timer to 15 minutes. Release the pressure over 10 minutes. Prepare the burgers using the vegetables.
- Serve with the fries and cola!

Nutrition (Per Serving):

Calories: 141; Fat: 34g; Carbohydrates: 93g; Protein: 19g

Pumpkin with Spices

Serving: 3
Prep Time: 15 minutes
Cooking Time: 40 minutes

Ingredients:

1. 20 oz pumpkin, sliced
2. 4 cherry tomatoes
3. 4 tablespoons Olive oil
4. 5 garlic cloves, minced
5. 3 teaspoons rosemary, dried
6. 2 teaspoons black pepper
7. 1 cup of water or vegetable broth
8. 1 teaspoon sea salt
9. 1 teaspoon nutmeg
10. 1 teaspoon basil, dried

How to Prepare:

- In a bowl, combine the black pepper, dried rosemary and garlic. Toss the pumpkin in the spices mix. Then set the pumpkin aside to marinate it for at least few hours unrefrigerated at room temperature.
- Combine all the ingredients in your Instant Pot and close the lid to let them cook on a MEDIUM pressure for 40 minutes.
- Release the pressure. Then divide the pumpkin into four bowls or plates and ladle up the sauce (if any). Serve with the white bread and wine.

Nutrition (Per Serving):

Calories: 156; Fat: 29g; Carbohydrates: 121g; Protein: 22g

THANK YOU

Thank you for choosing *Authentic Instant Pot Recipes* for improving your cooking skills! I hope you enjoyed the recipes while making them and tasting them! If you're interested in learning new recipes and new meals to cook, go and check out the other books of the serie.

CPSIA information can be obtained
at www.ICGtesting.com
Printed in the USA
BVHW091936060521
606647BV00006B/1123

9 781802 674361